SPEECH AND HEARING

A CAREER

KHYATI GUPTA

Copyright © Khyati Gupta
All Rights Reserved.

I would like to dedicate this book to late Mrs Nirajana Gupta , my dearest and lovable

person , my mother . She was a the light of hope in a dark tunnel. There are no words

which can describe her. when i completed my college , i was lost in the woods.

It was her who showed me this way of starting up my own clinic alas ! she isnt here to

see me grow with it. Her words and blessings will always stay with us.

Here is a message for you Mom . Even if you are not present physically here with

i feel your presence everywhere and you are tghe one still holding us and our fmaily together .

Contents

Foreword

Being an audiologist and Speech therapist in India. I face a lot of questions like

What is it about ? OR What actually do you deal with . people say they have not heard

about this before it is new for them. So I decided to give a brief as much as i can in this book

it is informative content about from this speech and hearing can create a whole medical career out of it

starting from communication its components types and then disorders.

I am hoping i have answered a few questions atleast .

do give it a try also it is a very good choice if you arfe looking for options to opt to build

your career . I say must go for it

1

INTRODUCTION

Hello there

Have you ever wondered

How do we connect to other living beings on earth .

Yes?

Well the answer to this question is not just very common but it is also something we knowingly or unknowingly do everyday with each other that is COMMUNICATE!

Now lets see what is communication

Communication basically is exchanging information through any of the means which help do it.

Communication originates from the Latin word communicare, meaning "to share" or "to be in re it is also an apparent answer to the painful divisions between self and other, private and public, and inner thought and outer world. Many scientists described and conceptualised communication in different ways as to define it is not only difficult but limits the definition in consistent manner.

There have been different models to define communication for example

In Claude Shannon's and Warren Weaver 's influential model, human communication was imagined to function like a telephone or telegraph. Accordingly, they conceptualized communication as involving discrete steps:

1.

The formation of communicative motivation or reason.

2.

Message composition further internal or technical elaboration on what exactly to express.

3.

Message encoding (for example, into digital data, written text, speech and so on).

4.

Transmission of the encoded message as a sequence of signals using a specific channel or medium.

5.

Noise sources such as natural forces and in some cases human activity (both intentional and accidental) begin influencing the quality of signals propagating from the sender to one or more receivers.

6.

Reception of signals and reassembling of the encoded message from a sequence of received signals.

7.

Decoding of the reassembled encoded message.

8.

Interpretation and _making sense_ of the _presumed_ original message.

Those include writing, speaking, talking, and, texting in today's digital world.

PART ONE

The Scientific study of communication can be divided into:

.

Information theory which studies the quantification, storage, and communication of information in general;

.

Communication studies which concerns human communication;

.

biosemiotics which examines communication in and between living organisms in general.

Biocommunication which exemplifies sign-mediated interactions in and between organisms of all domains of life, including viruses.

PART TWO

Well communication not only restricts to this we also communicate through our eyes, expressions and body language.

Not only humans but other living beings communicate too. Every being has some or the other methods, signs or signals of communicating with other members of the same species or family as we may say.

For example the honey bees have different shapes in which they move to indicate the distance of the nector from their hives.

This type of communication is called non verbal communication. The communication done by means of gestures, signs, symbols, face expressions, body language is included in this type of communication.

Lets learn more about non verbal communication

It conveys a type of information which is in a form of non-linguistic representation.

Some types are

Haptic communication which is a _branch of nonverbal communication that refers to the ways in which people and animals communicate and interact via the sense of touch. Touch is the most sophisticated and intimate of the five senses. Touch or haptics, from the ancient Greek word_

Chronemic communication which is a role of time in communication.

Others _gestures_, _body language_, _facial expressions_, _eye contact_ etc

Another factor of Nonverbal communication is that it also relates to the intent of a message. Some of the examples of intent are voluntary and some are involuntary , intentional movements like shaking a hand or winking are voluntary, as well as , sweating is involuntary. Speech which is a means of verbal communication which we will talk about later is also contains nonverbal elements known as paralanguage e.g. rhythm, intonation, tempo and stress. It affects communication most at the subconscious level and establishes trust. Likewise, written texts include nonverbal elements such as handwriting style, the spatial arrangement of words and the use of emoticons to convey emotion.

PART THREE

Now, the other type of communication is verbal.

It is the spoken or written form of a message.

A very important part of spoken or written communication is language which is defined as a system of symbols and the rules by which the symbols are manipulated which we know as the grammar

.

. <u>Language learning</u> normally occurs most intensively during human childhood. Most of the large number of human languages use patterns of <u>sound</u> or <u>gesture</u> for symbols which enable communication with others around them. Languages tend to share

certain properties, although there are exceptions.

2

LINGUISTICS

Linguistics

The study of human languages is called linguistics.

Linguistics plays an important role in verbal communication. As we all know verbal communication is mainly interjected through spoken or written language.

There are around more than 7000 human languages in the world.

Study of languages tell us that every language has certain signs and symbols to represent it while using a particular set of rules which we call as grammar.

Different branches in linguistics are

Phonology – the abstract sound system of a particular language

Morphology – structure of words

Syntax – the rules which govern the structure of sentences

Semantics – which is meaning of the words and sentences

Pragmatics – how social context contributes to the meaning

There are many branches in linguistics such as

psycholinguistics which is the study of how psychological factors are a part of human language.

Neurolinguistics – study of how human brain acquires, comprehends and expresses language .

And so many more.

3
SPEECH AND HEARING

SPEECH AND HEARING

So now I would like you to ponder upon a question what is it that humans have and no other species got ?

The answer is not language or communication as I have mentioned earlier that all organisms communicate in their own way .

SPEECH is something which is an main and important component of verbal language which is the gift only humans have !

17

I am here to discuss about a health-related paramedical field which is called Audiology and speech language pathology also known as the science of Speech and Hearing.

WHAT IS SPEECH AND HEARING

What is speech and hearing?

Speech and hearing can be defined as biological function in a human body which is controlled by brain specific organs of the human body such as larynx for speech and cochlea for hearing.

Speech, hereby is defines as expressing feelings or thoughts by using the articulatory organs Which shape the sounds using the exhaled breath from the lungs when passed through vocal cords present in larynx. The vocal cords are a v shaped muscular structure which has the ability to vibrate when the air passes through it. Vocal cords are present in larynx hence called the voice box. Voice which is shaped by the articulators to form sounds, sounds which when combined in a particular manner form meaningful words which is a result of speech.

What are articulators

Articulators are the organs which are situated in the mouth. For example, teeth, tongue, lips and palate. Articulators can be of two types that is passive articulators and active articulators. Passive articulators are the articulators which do not have the ability to move such as teeth, palate and lips. Active articulators are the ones which have the ability to move such as tongue. Any kind of abnormality in articulation causes disorder in speech which is called misarticulation.

Other types of speech disorders are stuttering, apraxia and dysarthria. The professionals who treat speech disorders are called speech therapist There are language disorders also in the occurrence which are treated by speech and language therapist too.

Hearing. What is hearing?

Recognizing the presence of sound with the help of specified organs present in a human body is called hearing. The organ involved in hearing are ear pinna ear canal and cochlea. The ear is responsible for hearing as well as balance. Cochlear part is responsible for hearing while the middle ear and vestibular *system in it are responsible for balance of human body.*

The sound is measured in Decibels. And any kind of abnormality in the cochlea to recognize the loudness of sound causes hearing disorder also called as hearing loss. Hearing ability is measured by an instrument called audiometer and kind of loss in the ability of hearing by the cochlea is called hearing loss. Hearing loss is measured in degrees such as minimal, mild, moderate, severe, very severe and profound.

The professionals who diagnose and treat hearing loss are called audiologist.

Audiologists also diagnose and treat other brain processing disorders such as central auditory processing disorder and also balance disorders.

PART TWO

As we read there are so many factors related to speech, language and hearing

,any impairment in speech, language or hearing can cause a faulty communication making the human having it differently abled from the rest of the humans

Speech therapist and audiologists are the right professionals to diagnose this and provide a appropriate treatment plan for such cases

We won't go in very deep about the disorders. There are plenty of disorders related to this which can be and have a rehabilitation.

Audiology and speech language pathology is a field where treatment and rehabilitation for such disorders or disabilities is practised. Different instruments and tools are used to diagnose these disorders such as audiologist use an audiometer to calculate the degree of hearing aid and prescribe hearing aids accordingly. speech therapist have questionnaires which are standard tools to diagnose speech related disorders such as Stuttering misarticulation

Even there are software's such as DR speech to diagnose voice weather it is harsh , breathy, or hoarse. And treatment is provided through therapy for the same.

Below are some pictures of the instatements used .

PART THREE

Hearing Aids are used for people with hearing impairment

Some people cant hear from birth

Some develop hearing loss later in life

All this impairments are treated with either cochlear implant specially recommended for congenital hearing loss which is by birth.

And hearing aids. The technology in hearing aids has also developed a lot the aids can be programmed according to the individuals requirement while connecting it with a software which gives a better and natural hearing experience.

These days hearing aid can also be connected to your mobile phones.

It is has a lot of scope and good opportunities. I myself being an audiologist and speech therapist feel proud to be in practise of the same.

There are many such aids for speech as well . For example Babies born with cleft lift and palate require feeding aids . which are bottles made to ease their drinking .

there speech tools as well which help in tongue massage to strenghthen muscles for speech

tools are also developed for augmentative and alternative communication which is a whole

lot of branch of this feild . It helps people with severe impairment to ease out their communication.

This was a brief about speech and hearing as a career

$$At\ Last$$

It has been a benevolent adventure being in the profession of speech therapy

and audiology. There is plenty you can learn and yet more to explore

THANK YOU
HAPPY READING
KHYATI GUPTA